SCIENTIFIC
AMERICAN

Weather, and How It Works

SCIENTIFIC
AMERICAN

Weather, and How It Works

By Randi Mehling

An imprint of Infobase Publishing

Scientific American: Weather, and How It Works

© 2007 by Infobase Publishing

Scientific American is a registered trademark of Scientific American, Inc. Its use is pursuant to a license with Scientific American, Inc.

Chelsea House
An imprint of Infobase Publishing
132 West 31st Street
New York, NY 10001

ISBN-10: 0-7910-9053-1

ISBN-13: 978-0-7910-9053-4

Library of Congress Cataloging-in-Publication Data
Mehling, Randi.
  Weather, and how it works / Randi Mehling.
      p. cm. — (Scientific American)
  Includes bibliographical references and index.
  ISBN 0-7910-9053-1
  1. Weather—Juvenile literature. I. Title. II. Series: Scientific American
(Chelsea House Publishers)
  QC981.3.M49 2006
  551.6—dc22   2006014850

Chelsea House books are available at special discounts when purchased in bulk quantities for businesses, associations, institutions, or sales promotions. Please call our Special Sales Department in New York at (212) 967-8800 or (800) 322-8755.

You can find Chelsea House books on the World Wide Web at http://www.chelseahouse.com

Series designed by Gilda Hannah
Cover designed by Takeshi Takahashi

Printed in the United States of America

Bang GH 10 9 8 7 6 5 4 3 2 1

This book is printed on acid-free paper.

All links and Web addresses were checked and verified to be correct at the time of publication. Because of the dynamic nature of the Web, some addresses and links may have changed since publication and may no longer be valid.

Contents

CHAPTER ONE

Weather: You Like It or Not

Across the flat prairies of Kansas, lightning strikes the ground with a zigzag bolt of electricity. A few seconds later, thunder booms. Hailstones fall from the sky, cooling off this hot, humid summer day in mid-August. Some are as big as golf balls and dent cars upon impact.

In the Florida Keys, it is hurricane season, and an 85-mile-per-hour (137-kilometer) wind tears off roofs, floods streets, and knocks down telephone poles.

In January, a blinding blizzard in northern Michigan forces all transportation to a halt, dumping three feet of snow in some places. Winds pile up snowdrifts that cover most parked cars. Meanwhile, in the Southern Hemisphere, January is summertime in Australia, and it is a sunny Saturday in the upper eighties. Thousands of people have flocked to the beach to enjoy the beautiful weather.

What do all these scenes have in common? They describe the weather. Since the earliest of humankind's days on the planet, we have tried to make sense of the outdoor conditions of rain, sun, sleet, hail, wind, and snow. It seems as if the world goes crazy during hurricanes, tornados, and thunderous **storms**. There is no escaping the weather—it affects every aspect of our lives.

Hurricane winds have been known to rip coconuts off palm trees and send them flying through the air at high speeds. That's another reason to stay inside during a hurricane!

Every living creature on Earth depends upon the weather for its survival. Farmers depend upon rain to grow the food we eat. Schools close when it snows a lot, and planes cannot depart with ice on their wings. Without water from rain and snow, life would not exist on the planet. Sailboats use wind to travel around the world. We even choose which clothes to wear based on the weather. It is no wonder the most common conversation between two people, in any country and in any language, is about the weather and what it might do next.

Weather happens, whether we want it to or not. It is completely uncontrollable and often takes us by surprise. Do you know of anyone who can stand outside and tell a thunderstorm to stop raining or redirect the wind to blow somewhere else? Because it is so vital to our everyday life, people have always tried to understand and predict the weather. By knowing the weather ahead of time, we can better prepare for it. We carry an umbrella when rain is forecast. We postpone a trip if a major storm is brewing. Farmers might plant extra rows of crops in anticipation of a wet growing season. Sailors might travel a different route to avoid a storm or to take advantage of strong sailing winds.

Nature Forecasts the Weather

The first humans did not have thermometers, weather satellites, The Weather Channel, or the Internet. Instead, the first weather forecaster on the planet was nature. People observed the world

CAN PINECONES PREDICT THE WEATHER?

Pinecones have traditionally been used to forecast the weather. Their shape changes depending on the moisture in the **air**. They open up in dry weather and close in damp weather. The petals of the morning glory flower act in a similar way. It has been observed that the flower shuts its petals before rain and bad weather and opens its petals for fine weather. Scientific evidence has proved that these are indeed reliable and useful weather indicators.

If morning glory flowers open their petals, it will most likely be a sunny day.

around them and noticed that nature provided many clues about the weather. Plants and animals behaved differently before certain weather events and so informed us of what type of weather to expect. People predicted the weather based on these signs from nature but never with 100% accuracy. However, these natural patterns occurred often enough for people to believe in them.

Passed along from generation to generation, these signs of weather eventually become known as weather folklore—well-known sayings that people use all the time to forecast the weather. There are literally hundreds of these weather predictions based on nature. Weather folklore relies on patterns observed over a long time, not scientific measurement. However, it is very interesting to note that scientific methods have proved that many of these natural forecasts are true.

The weather is about as easy to predict as giving your cat a bubble bath. Even today, with high-tech science, we cannot predict the weather with complete accuracy. Many people all over the world choose to combine modern scientific technology with the signs that nature provides to give them the best possible weather forecast.

Ancient Ideas About Weather

Archaeologists, who study ancient civilizations, tell us that the people from those times—more than 4,000 or 5,000 years ago—believed gods were responsible for the whims of weather. A different god was in control of a particular aspect of the weather, such as rain, wind, or thunder. Weather does seem magical. It is always changing, and we know it is uncontrollable. Weather helps us sometimes, and other times it causes us tremendous harm. For instance, rain helps to nourish fruits, vegetables, and grains. It provides us with water to drink. Yet, other times rain has the power to devastate. It can be accompanied by lightning, which can strike and kill a person. Rain can cause flash **floods,** which can wash out an entire town.

Many indigenous people in the United States and throughout the world perform rain ceremonies. In these ceremonies, people of all ages participate in songs, dances, rituals, and prayers, just as their ancestors did hundreds or even thousands of years ago.

In order to explain these positive and negative experiences of nature, ancient cultures and civilizations intertwined religion with the weather. Most thought supreme beings (in the forms of gods and goddesses) had the power of life and death over them and lived in fear of offending the gods. An angry god might create a long-lasting drought, causing crops to die. People and animals would go thirsty and hungry; many would die.

These civilizations created many rituals in which ceremonial offerings were made to please the gods. Grains and jewelry were offered, and it was common to sacrifice animals and even, sometimes, humans. In exchange for the people's devotion to their gods, it was believed that they would be rewarded with bountiful crops and prosperity.

Gods of Thunder and Sky

The Incas worshipped many gods and goddesses. Each one was connected to a type of weather. For instance, the Incas prayed to their rain god Apu Illapu when they needed rain. They believed he drew water from the Milky Way and then poured it down on Earth as rain. Even in modern times, there are still many Inca descendants living in Peru who worship the original Inca gods.

THE THUNDERBIRD

The thunderbird is a very important mythical figure in Native American cultures. Living high in the mountains, the thunderbird flaps its wings, making the sky shake with thunder. When the thunderbird blinks or looks down, lightning shoots out of its eyes and hits the ground. Tribes in the Pacific Northwest have a thunderbird to protect them and often carve its figure on the top of totem poles.

Animals, figures, and shapes are carved in a specific order on totem poles, which can be more than 40 feet (12 m) high. The designs shown on the totem pole above tell stories or legends about the Indians who lived around Vancouver, Canada.

The ancient Maya believed gods controlled the natural elements of water, wind, fire, and earth. Chac is a benevolent Maya rain god who, as the legend goes, had a frog orchestra (because frogs are thought to be calling the rain when they croak). Today, modern ancestors of the Maya, the people of Yucatán, Mexico, still refer to Chac when they want it to rain.

In Norse mythology, Thor is the god of thunder and sky. Legend tells how he chased away the frost. The rolling wheels of Thor's chariot rumbled like thunder, and he hurled his mighty hammer like a lightning bolt at "the frost giants." Thor is credited with the return of warm spring rains to the land.

Revealing the Mystery Behind Weather

The Greek philosopher Aristotle wrote a book around 340 B.C. called *Meteorologica*. In it, he explained his ideas on such weather-related topics as clouds, wind, lightning, snow, and climate change from a philosophical, not a scientific, point of view. Interestingly, Aristotle's ideas on these natural forces and their relationships to each other were thought to be true for about 2,000 years.

Toward the end of the sixteenth century, scientific instruments that could measure characteristics of the weather were invented. Because of this new scientific data, the majority of Aristotle's ideas were disproved. However, some of Aristotle's conclusions were proved correct, perhaps showing us that the best scientific tool is an observant, analytical mind. Today we use the word *meteorology* to describe the science of weather and weather forecasting.

Several important achievements occurred during the scientific revolution of the sixteenth and seventeenth centuries. These discoveries shaped our knowledge of **meteorology** and continue to help us understand the weather even today in the twenty-first century. Italian architect Leon Battista Alberti invented the first mechanical wind vane in 1450. This gave us the ability to tell the direction of the wind. Galileo Galilei invented the **thermometer** around 1593, allowing the measurement of temperatures. Evangelista Torricelli's **barometer** was invented in 1643 and measured the weight of air—also known as **air pressure**. Because of these scientific inventions, we now know that changes in temperature and air pressure create the wind that powers our weather.

Evangelista Torricelli built the first mercury barometer in 1644. Also known as Torricelli's Tube, this invention allowed scientists to measure the pressure of the atmosphere.

Instruments that measured meteorological data continued to develop during the eighteenth and nineteenth centuries. Scientists soon learned that different locations around the world experienced different types of weather conditions. Yet a scientist in Italy had to wait weeks or possibly months to get news of weather in the United States. Even within the United States, it took a long time to share this exciting weather information.

The widespread use of the telegraph by 1843 changed that. No matter where researchers were living, the weather happening right then and there was recorded and transmitted to a central location. The telegraph allowed scientists to create the first weather maps of the entire world. For the first time, scientists could track how the weather on one side of the world affected weather around the globe.

Today, meteorological scientists know that weather is a mixture of the air we breathe, the **Sun**'s energy, the rotation of Earth, and the movement of water and wind. Technologies such as Doppler radar and satellites assist meteorologists as they continue to unravel the deep mysteries of the weather.

CHAPTER TWO

The Air We Breathe

Take a deep breath. The air you breathe makes up the weather. The term *weather* describes what the air is doing in any particular time and place. For instance, the air can be warm, cold, wet, dry, calm, or windy, depending upon where you are in the world.

The **climate** describes the typical weather of a geographic area on Earth. For example, the climate in Antarctica is very cold, whereas in the tropics, such as Tahiti, the climate is very hot. We know these climates are typical because the weather patterns there have not changed for a long, long time. Climate can be very different, even if two regions are close in distance. It could be snowing on top of a mountain, and in the valley below it could be raining.

We feel the sensation of the air on our skin each day and choose our clothes to either stay warm or cool. However, where does air come from? We know we need oxygen to breathe, but what else is air made of? Let's begin at the beginning—the birth of our planet.

As viewed from space, a protective layer of atmosphere surrounds our planet Earth.

It's a Gas

About 4.5 billion years ago, the planets in the solar system formed from the dust and gas that surrounded the Sun. The two most abundant elements in the universe are helium and hydrogen. These gases cloaked the newly formed planets like a protective blanket. This is called an **atmosphere**. However, Earth's gravity was not strong enough to hold onto this new atmosphere, and these gases floated back into space. The other planets that orbited close to the Sun—Venus, Mars, and Mercury —could not retain their atmospheres either.

Then something amazing happened on Earth. Our planet created its own atmosphere. At its center, Earth was extremely hot and unstable. All over the world, gigantic volcanic eruptions ripped through the surface of the planet, bringing elements from its core to the surface. Water, carbon dioxide, methane, sul-

This specially-photographed image shows pollution over New York City. Scientists have linked increases in childhood asthma to air pollution.

fur, and nitrogen filled the empty space around Earth. This time the atmosphere stayed put. Earth's gravity was strong enough to hold these gases to the planet.

Our air was born. There was just one thing missing: oxygen. Nothing alive today would be able to breathe this toxic brew of steam, sulfurous clouds, and carbon dioxide. The whole world probably smelled like a rotten egg (which releases sulfur).

Luckily, life did evolve under these circumstances. About one billion years ago, plants began to photosynthesize. They released oxygen into the atmosphere. Ozone (three oxygen atoms) formed from oxygen gas (two oxygen atoms) and floated about 10 to 20 miles up in the sky. This ozone layer absorbed the intense ultraviolet (UV) rays from the Sun, protecting the plant life. Plants flourished, and more oxygen went into the atmosphere surrounding the planet. Eventually there was enough oxygen to support oxygen-breathing animals such as dinosaurs and mammals, including humans.

The Protective Shield—Our Atmosphere

The main ingredient in our air is nitrogen (about 78%). Oxygen makes up the next biggest portion, forming about 21%. The remaining 1% of our atmosphere contains trace amounts of other gases, including carbon dioxide, hydrogen, argon, helium, neon, krypton, xenon, and water vapor—water in its gaseous form.

These gases constantly mix and swirl together to form our air, which sustains all life on Earth. The atmosphere is made up of

TESTING THE WEIGHT OF AIR

Tie a piece of string in the middle of a stick so that it balances when you hold the string. Tie an empty balloon to each end of the stick. The two balloons should balance evenly. Now, untie one balloon and blow air into it. Tie the blown-up balloon back onto one end of the stick. The end with the blown-up balloon should dip downward. The balloon filled with air is heavier than the empty one.

five layers, like blankets piled on top of each other. The blanket closest to Earth is the heaviest and contains the most air. As you move higher into the sky, the blankets get lighter and lighter. This is because the higher you go, the less air there is.

The layers act like a protective shield. They maintain a comfortable **temperature** on Earth. Without an atmosphere, we would be burnt to a crisp by the powerful heat of the Sun during the day or **freeze** to death during the cold night.

Ozone, carbon dioxide, and water make up only a tiny portion of our air, less than 1%. However, they have very important jobs:

SUNNY FACTS

- The Sun is the largest object in the solar system.
- More than one million Earths can fit inside the Sun.
- The Sun is approximately 4.5 billion years old and is roughly half way through its lifespan, estimated at 10 billion years.
- Scientists predict that in about 4 to 5 billion years, the Sun will begin to run out of its hydrogen fuel and swell up to 100 times its present size.
- When the Sun expands, scientists theorize that the inner planets, including Earth, will be engulfed and destroyed.

Even though the Sun is 93 million miles (150 million km) from Earth, it powers our world with infrared light. This energy is absorbed in the troposphere and provides us with most of our heat.

they all protect life on Earth. The ozone layer in our atmosphere acts like a filter. It blocks the Sun's harmful UV rays 20 miles (32 km) above our heads. Without the ozone layer to protect us, the UV rays would be too intense for life to survive. Carbon dioxide provides food for plant photosynthesis. Water, with assistance from the Sun, provides us with all the different types of weather we have here on Earth, such as clouds, rain, and snow.

Layers of the Atmosphere

Remember that the layers of the atmosphere are held around the planet by the force of gravity. The layer of air closest to the ground is called the troposphere. It extends about 7 miles (11 km) up from the ground. All weather happens in this layer because it contains most of the water vapor in the air. Most clouds form in this layer.

In general, as you move higher into the sky, each layer of the atmosphere gets progressively colder. This is because Earth absorbs the heat from the Sun faster than the air does. It makes sense that the troposphere is the warmest layer of the atmosphere. It is the layer closest to Earth. The higher you go in the sky, or the greater your altitude, the colder it gets.

The second layer of air above Earth's surface is the stratosphere, which extends from about 7 to 31 miles (11–50 km) in the sky. Ozone is found in the stratosphere. Because ozone absorbs high-energy UV rays from the Sun, this layer is actually warmer than the troposphere. The presence of ozone creates a

Clouds form in the troposphere, where airlines fly. A balloon floats above in the stratosphere; meteor showers (*lower center*) occur in the mesosphere. The space shuttle and aurora lights are above in the thermosphere. Different kinds of electromagnetic radiation (*left to right*) penetrate the atmosphere: gamma rays, X-rays, ultraviolet rays, a rainbow of visible light, and radiowaves.

special exception to the rule that it gets colder as you move higher into the sky.

The mesosphere is the third layer of atmosphere above the ground. The air here is very cold, and temperatures can average –100°F (–73°C). The altitude of this layer is between about 31 and 50 miles (50 and 80 km) up in the sky. The higher you travel, the less air there is. Scientists say the air "thins" as you travel up toward space.

The fourth and fifth layers of the atmosphere are found at very high altitudes. The thermosphere is about 50 miles (80 km) above Earth. Astronauts and space shuttles travel in this layer of the atmosphere. Once you are up beyond 300 miles (480 km), you are in the fifth layer, the exosphere. Weather satellites are located in this layer. The upper limit of Earth's atmosphere is about 6,200 miles (10,000 km) in the sky. At this point, there is hardly any air left. What little air remains in the exosphere layer escapes Earth's gravity and floats into space.

CHAPTER THREE

A Hot World Under Pressure

The gases that make up our air are constantly moving, mixing, and churning in every direction, like soup simmering in a pot. They get their energy from the Sun. Sunlight warms the temperature of the air above Earth and sets these gases in motion.

However, there is more to the story. Earth rotates every 24 hours on its axis. This spinning of the planet also contributes greatly to the movement of air. The movements of air create all the different types of weather we know, including wind, rain, and sunny days. Let's explore how air moves.

Gravity Keeps Us Grounded

Gravity is the force that pulls everything toward the ground. Humans, dogs, trees, buildings, clouds, and the gases in our atmosphere are all held to the earth because of gravity. Without this invisible hold on us, we would be weightless and drift above the ground. The planet would have no atmosphere because the gases would just drift out to space.

Gravity gives everything a certain weight. The weight of your body puts pressure on loose dirt and leaves a footprint. The more you weigh, the more you push on the ground and the deeper the footprint you leave.

Air also presses down on Earth's surface because it has a certain weight. Its weight is known as air pressure. Air pressure is always changing. It weighs more in some geographic areas, called **high-pressure** regions, and less in other places, called **low-pressure** regions. A barometer is one tool used to measure the weight of air.

Air travels like water in a river. It naturally flows from areas of high pressure to areas of low pressure. The difference between high- and low-pressure areas is one of the main reasons we have any weather at all. Still, how exactly does air put pressure on us?

The Highs and Lows of Pressure

Although we are not aware of it, the gases in our atmosphere are made of trillions of molecules bouncing around, bumping and pushing into each other. For example, oxygen is a molecule. Nitrogen is a molecule. Carbon dioxide is a molecule. These air molecules are constantly moving up, down, sideways, and diagonally—like ping-pong balls in a clothes dryer.

If you were an air molecule, you might feel like you were being pelted with snowballs your whole life. Each time another molecule crashed into you, you would feel its impact on your body. Scientists gauge the pressure of air by measuring the number of these impacts.

TESTING AIR FLOW

Take the balloon that was full of air from the experiment you did in Chapter Two. When you filled the balloon with air, the increasing air pressure expanded the sides of the balloon. The air pressure inside it is high. Now, untie the balloon, and let the air out. What happens? The air immediately flows from inside the balloon to outside the balloon, where the air pressure is lower.

Wind turbines harness the power of the wind instead of fossil fuels to generate electricity. A wind farm is a bunch of wind turbines in one location.

The more air there is, the more air weighs, just as the more of you there is, the more you weigh. The more air weighs, the more impacts there are. This all means higher air pressure. Less air means there will be less frequent impacts. Therefore, the air pressure is lower since the air weighs less. Air pressure is the weight of all the air molecules pushing down on the ground.

Let us now see how we can personally tell how much air weighs, without using any scientific instruments or training.

The Weight of the World

The weight of air is the heaviest at the surface of our planet because most of our air is located there. Scientists measure the weight of air on the surface at 14.7 pounds (6.7 kg) per square

A barometer measures changes in atmospheric pressure and is used to forecast the weather.

Mount Everest rises more than 29,000 feet (8,849 m) above sea level. The farther away you are from sea level, the less air there is. At the top there is only one third of the amount of oxygen found at its base, so most climbers need an extra supply of oxygen to reach the summit.

inch. This means that the amount of air molecules pressing down on one square inch weighs 14.7 pounds. It is like an invisible hand pressing down on everything and everyone.

You don't notice this pressure until you move to a higher altitude. Air pressure becomes lighter and lighter the higher you go because air thins—there are fewer air molecules—as the altitude increases. If you hike up to the top of a mountain, there is less air there than on the ground. This includes oxygen, a major part of air. So, the higher you climb, the harder it is to breathe.

At 18,000 feet (5,486 m) above the ground, there is much less air pushing down. Because there is less air pushing down, there

In 1742, Anders Celsius was credited with inventing the Celsius temperature scale, which measures the freezing point of water at 0° and its boiling point at 100°. On the Fahrenheit temperature scale, water freezes at 32° and boils at 212°.

In 1714, Gabriel Daniel Fahrenheit improved upon Galileo's earlier design (a water thermometer) by constructing a mercury thermometer. The Fahrenheit scale was the first reliable way of measuring temperature. Water freezes just below 32 degrees Fahrenheit, it melts just above 32 degrees, and it boils at 212 degrees. Here in the United States, we still measure temperature in degrees Fahrenheit. However, the worldwide scientific community uses the Celsius scale to measure temperature.

In 1742, the Swedish astronomer Anders Celsius proposed a new scale for thermometers. Another scientist named Jean-Pierre Christin made additional improvements to the Celsius scale in 1743. Water freezes at 0 degrees Celsius, and it boils at 100 degrees Celsius.

CONVERSION OF FAHRENHEIT AND CELSIUS
• To convert from °F (degrees Fahrenheit) to °C (degrees Celsius): Take the temperature in Fahrenheit, and subtract 32 from it. Then, multiply that number by 5 and divide it by 9.
• To convert from °C to °F: Take the temperature in Celsius and multiply it by 9. Then, divide that number by 5 and add 32 to it.

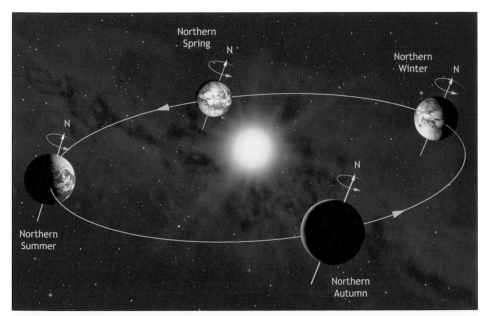

Earth takes 365¼ days—one year—to orbit the Sun. Because Earth is tilted during its orbit, each area receives different amounts of the Sun's energy at different times of the year. This is why we have seasons.

is less weight, or air pressure, as well. The air at this altitude is measured at 7.3 pounds (3.3 kg) per square inch. That is almost half the weight of air measured at the surface! At this altitude, about half of all our atmosphere's air molecules are below you and about half are above you. Mountain climbers can feel light-headed, dizzy, and nauseous at these high altitudes. They often wear masks connected to oxygen tanks to help them breathe. This allows them to avoid the symptoms of what is known as altitude sickness.

As you fly up through the five layers of the atmosphere, the air pressure eventually becomes zero. There is no longer any air left to exert any downward pressure.

The Sun Moves the Air

How air moves is a whole other story. Weather is created by changes in air pressure and temperature. The temperature gets the whole process started.

The Sun's rays go through the atmosphere and hit Earth's surface. This energy heats the land and the oceans. As the surface warms up, heat rises and warms the air right above the surface. The hotter the air gets, the faster the molecules bounce around. The faster the warming air moves, the more its air pressure increases.

As the air along the ground warms from the Sun, the air above it remains cool. This cooler air also moves more slowly than warm air. Because the cold air is found higher in the sky than warm air, and because it moves more slowly than warm air, cooler air has a lower air pressure than warmer air.

Since air flows from high to low pressure, the warm air rises toward the cold air. Warm air is lighter than cold air. Like a balloon, it rises higher and higher. Warm air gets colder as it rises.

At the same time, cold air sinks because it is heavier than warm air. As it sinks closer to the ground, the cold air begins to warm up. Directly above the ground the cold air is now completely warmed by the heat of Earth's surface. It begins to rise toward the cooler air. The air continues to trade places in an endless cycle of circulation around the whole world.

Balancing Act

Yet, Earth does not heat up evenly. Some areas of the world, like the tropics (near the **equator**), are much hotter all year round than, say, the extremely cold areas near the North and South

NIGHT AND DAY

Earth's position in relation to the Sun is always changing. The planet spins around its axis, an imaginary line that runs between the North and South Poles. One complete spin takes 24 hours. This is why half of Earth is lit and warm (daytime), while the other half faces away from the Sun (nighttime). At the North Pole the Sun doesn't set at all in the weeks surrounding June 21 (the Summer Solstice), whereas the South Pole lies in continual darkness. The reverse is true in the weeks surrounding the Winter Solstice (December 21).

poles. Because Earth rotates, the warm air and the cold air are stirred up. This continuous movement of warm and cold air is like a giant fan. It transfers heat from hot areas of the world to cold areas. This worldwide air circulation helps Earth keep its temperature in balance.

However, there are vast temperature differences between the equator and the North and South poles. Air circulation cannot balance these extreme temperatures. It never completely cools down in the tropics, and the poles never warm up. Therefore, the tropics always have a surplus of heat, and the poles always have a surplus of cold.

These temperature differences between the equator and the North and South poles are the reason we have weather. They are the reason the air in the atmosphere will always be flowing from high to low pressure. The hot air over the equator rises toward the poles, replacing the cooler polar air. This cooler air sinks toward the ground, flowing toward the equator. In doing so, these air movements—also known as winds—help create the world's weather.

CHAPTER FOUR

It's All About Water

Floods, thunderstorms, clouds, rivers, lakes, swimming pools, snowballs, puddles, baths, ice cubes, and hot tea. What do they all have in common? Water.

Water takes up less than 1% of the atmosphere. Yet, without water, nothing could live on the planet. If water did not exist, there would be no swimming, fishing, or snowboarding. Plus, regular bathing would be difficult.

The Water Cycle

Oceans, lakes, rivers, and streams cover about 70% of Earth. The amount of water on Earth is finite—the amount never changes. However, the amount of water on Earth is always being recycled and changing what it looks like. Water can take on three different forms, depending on how hot or cold it is. When the temperature is above 32°F (0°C), water is a liquid. When it is colder than 32°F, water becomes block ice. When you boil liquid water, it becomes a gas called water vapor. This is also called steam.

As it changes through each of its three forms, water moves up into the sky and back down to the ground in a never-ending cycle called the water cycle. It is also known as the hydrologic cycle. *Hydro* means water.

Water is redistributed in a continuous cycle: evaporating from the ocean and the land and falling as precipitation; and flowing from the land to the ocean in rivers and streams.

Evaporation and Condensation

It takes a lot of energy to constantly change from a gas to a liquid to a solid. Sunshine provides this energy. The Sun's rays heat the oceans, lakes, and other bodies of water on the surface. As the water heats up, the liquid water becomes warm water vapor and forms part of the air. This process is called **evaporation**. We know how warm air moves—it rises into the sky. The amount of water vapor in the air is called humidity. Without knowing it, we are surrounded by water all the time in the air we breathe.

As the warm air rises, it begins to cool off the higher it goes. As the air becomes colder, the water vapor changes into drops of liquid. When lots of these drops accumulate, they form clouds,

mist, and **fog**. This is called **condensation**. Clouds are made up of billions of tiny water droplets. If it is cold enough, the water vapor condenses into ice. Clouds can also be made of ice crystals along with water droplets. Fog and mist are clouds that form near the ground instead of in the sky.

Water droplets can only condense when there is dust, smoke, or other tiny particles in the air. These particles are called condensation nuclei. They give the water vapor something to cling to in order to become a droplet. When there is a lot of pollution,

DO YOU KNOW ABOUT FROST?

Have you ever had to scrape frost off the windshield of a car? Frost forms when water vapor freezes into icy crystals on cold surfaces such as windows and trees. Dew is water vapor that condenses into drops of moisture during the cool night. You can see these dew drops on leaves, plants, and spider webs.

As the temperature drops, the moisture in the air condenses into dew. When the temperature reaches 32°F (0°C) this dew freezes into what we call frost.

Sunlight looks white, but it's really made up of different colors: red, orange, yellow, green, blue, indigo, and violet. The colors of a rainbow are always in the same order. The Sun makes rainbows when white sunlight passes through raindrops. To see a rainbow, the Sun must be shining behind you as you look toward the falling rain.

A popular way to remember the order of the colors of the rainbow is: ROY G. BIV. The letters stand for red, orange, yellow, green, blue, indigo, and violet.

there are more particles in the air, and therefore more clouds are able to form.

Water from the Sky

Without clouds, it would not rain. The tiny water droplets keep condensing, and they grow larger and larger within the clouds. When the water droplets are big enough, the clouds cannot contain them. They fall to the ground as rain, snow, or ice, depending on the temperature of the air below the clouds. Any type of water that falls from the sky is called **precipitation**. Precipitation is usually absorbed into the ground or falls into rivers and oceans.

Each snowflake is made of two to about two hundred separate crystals.

As the Sun heats the surface waters of the planet, water evaporates. This process of evaporation—and the water cycle—continues indefinitely.

Rain and Snow

The two most common types of precipitation are rain and snow. Rain can fall fast and furiously or light and gently. A **drizzle** is made of very fine raindrops. Sometimes streets flood and riverbanks overflow when heavy rainstorms dump large amounts of water on the ground in a short time. The **monsoon** season in Asia is famous for this. Countries like India are soaked by rains for six months of the year and are dry for the rest of the time. The people of this country are used to this weather pattern.

Snow is ice that falls from the sky. A snowflake forms when water vapor turns directly from a gas into ice without going through the liquid stage. This means the air in the cloud is below freezing. The tiny ice crystals stick together, just like a water droplet, until they are heavy enough to drop out of the cloud. However, as the snow falls through the air toward the ground, the air might be warmer than it was in the cloud. Then, the snow turns to rain before it hits the ground. If the air stays close to freezing, the snowflakes will not melt. It is common to see snow on top of a mountain, where the air is colder, while it is raining in the warmer valley below.

Hail and Sleet

When strong winds toss raindrops high inside clouds, they freeze into balls of ice called hail. These chunks of ice are flung up and down inside the cloud. Layers of ice build up and form a rounded hailstone. The largest hailstone on record in the United States had a diameter of 7 inches (18 cm) and weighed one pound (.5 kg). It was about the size of a cantaloupe melon and sped more than 100 miles (161 km) per hour as it fell from the sky. The heaviest hailstone in the United States was about 5.5 inches (14 cm) in diameter and weighed 1.67 pounds (.76 kg). The heaviest hailstone ever reported was in India and weighed 2.2 pounds (1.0 kg). Hail can be dangerous and cause crop and even building damage. Hailstones look like stones and feel like stones if they hit you on the head!

Sleet is falling ice that is smaller and wetter than hailstones. It feels like slush—water that is half liquid and half ice.

Clouds

Clouds can tell what the day's weather holds in store for you, based on their shape and size. There are three main types of clouds floating in the sky: cirrus, cumulus, and stratus.

SNOW AND RAIN ARE NOT THE SAME

Snow takes up about 10 times the space as rain. Because it takes up so much space, snow piles up quickly on the ground. You can test this: Collect some snow in a glass and mark its level. After it melts, mark the level of water in the glass. (By the way, it takes about one million cloud droplets to provide enough water for one raindrop.)

Cirrus clouds are thin, feathery, white, and wispy. Because they form high in the sky where it is very cold, they are made of ice crystals, not water droplets.

Cumulus clouds are puffy and usually mean fair weather. They have flat bottoms and hang low in the sky.

Cirrus clouds look feathery and wispy, and *cirrus* literally means "curl" in Latin. They form high in the sky where it is very cold, at around 18,000 to 40,000 feet (5,486–12,192 m). Because of this, they are made of ice crystals, not water droplets. The wind is responsible for blowing cirrus clouds into curls. These clouds are often called "mare's tails" because they look like the tail of a horse. Cirrus clouds often signal bad weather.

Those puffy clouds that look like cotton balls or cauliflower floating in the sky are called cumulus clouds. They form much lower—approximately 2,000 to 6,000 feet (610–1,829 m) above the ground. Cumulus clouds are made of tiny water droplets and are usually seen in fine weather against a blue sky.

If you see a wide sheet of gray, shapeless clouds very close to the ground, it is probably a stratus cloud. These clouds stretch in all directions and are often dark and gloomy. Light, misty rain and drizzle typically fall from stratus clouds. Fog is a type of stratus cloud.

Clouds also determine how hot or cold you feel. Clouds act as insulators. They prevent the flow of heat, so a hot day will feel even hotter if it's cloudy. A cloudy nighttime sky will also hold the heat of the day closer to the ground, so that the evening feels warmer. Conversely, a nighttime sky without any clouds will generally feel very chilly. There is nothing to keep the heat close to Earth's surface during the cold, sunless night.

Rain Clouds Predict Stormy Weather

Don't be fooled by sweet, fluffy cumulus clouds. Sometimes the sight of these clouds tells us the weather will be nice. Under certain weather conditions, though, cumulus clouds will group together and become rain clouds called cumulonimbus clouds. *Nimbus* means "rainstorm" in Latin.

Cumulonimbus clouds are distinctively larger and darker than cumulus clouds. They look gray or black. This is because they are

Harmless cumulus clouds can quickly develop into large towering cumulonimbus clouds, which are associated with powerful thunderstorms.

so full of water and ice crystals that sunlight cannot shine through them. They have the same puffy characteristics as cumulus clouds. However, cumulonimbus clouds build higher and more vertically into the sky-like towers. They often have flat tops, like a blacksmith's anvil. Some of these clouds measure more than 9 miles high (14 km)—taller than Mount Everest.

Cumulonimbus clouds usually bring rain, hail, and **thunder** with them. When you see these clouds, you can be sure of the weather forecast. They can become so large and powerful that they can dump as much as 3 feet (almost 1 m) of rain in one afternoon.

Thunderstorms and Forks of Lightning

When you notice a cumulus cloud change from a round shape to a rising tower, be warned. A **thunderstorm** is likely on its way. Thunderstorms often occur at the end of hot, sticky summer days. This is because the warm, moist air rises very quickly to form large cumulonimbus clouds. It is very windy inside these tall clouds. The water and ice in a cumulonimbus cloud bang against each other, and electricity builds up. Eventually the cloud releases this electricity as a flash of lightning.

Lightning always takes the quickest route to the ground, usually striking the tallest object around, such as a tree or building. This is why it is important to get to lower ground if you are hiking on a mountaintop. You do not want to be the tallest object around in a thunderstorm, and you do not want to be standing *near* the tallest tree either!

HOW FAR AWAY IS THAT THUNDERSTORM?

Count the number of seconds between seeing a flash of lightning and hearing the thunder. For every 5 seconds you count, the storm is about 1 mile (1.6 km) away from you. If the thunderstorm is close, the thunder will sound like a loud crack. A low, rumbling thunder means the storm is farther away. The closer the storm, the faster you should seek shelter from it!

Thunder and lightning actually happen at the same time. However, since light travels much faster than sound, we see lightning before we hear thunder.

As lightning strikes the ground, it heats the air around it. This has been measured at around five times the heat of the Sun, about 55,000°F (30,538°C). When the air gets this hot, it sounds like an explosion. The sound is called thunder. Thunder and lightning happen at the same time, but we see lightning before we hear thunder. This is because light travels at a much faster speed than sound.

When lightning hits the ground, it is called fork lightning. Lightning actually has two bolts. First, it zigzags to the ground from the cloud. A split second later, the lightning races up the exact route back to the cloud. Sheet lightning is lightning that flashes within the cloud itself.

CHAPTER FIVE

Windy, Wild Weather

Wind is air on the move, and it often creates dramatic weather. It can flutter your hair in a summer **breeze** or slap you across the face as a **blizzard** blinds you with snow or a hurricane rips the roof off your house. Strong winds can be scary and dangerous, but they can be exciting as well. For example, in 1999, scientists managed to put a Doppler radar *inside* an Oklahoma tornado and measured the fastest recorded wind speed of 318 miles (198 km) per hour.

Wind is described by its direction and speed. This allows meteorologists to track how fast and where a storm might hit in your area. The three main forces that affect wind are high and low air pressure, friction, and the rotation of our planet.

Pressuring Wind to Blow

Remember that Earth is heated unevenly. Warm, high-pressure air near the equator is always rising, and cold, low-pressure air from the North and South poles is always sinking. All air moves from areas of high pressure to areas of low pressure. This movement of air is the wind. A popular phrase to help you remember this is "Winds blow from high to low."

Friction

Compared to the ocean, the land is an obstacle course for wind. As the wind blows over land, it has to go over or around mountains, buildings, trees, and cars. These obstacles actually rub against the wind, causing friction. The force of friction either blocks or slows down the wind. You can notice this force when using your feet to slow down your speed on a bike. The friction between your feet and the road's surface is what slows your bike down. Over the ocean, there is only flat water, no obstacles. Winds over the oceans are much faster because of this, which is why high-speed winds like hurricanes begin over the oceans.

Coriolis Effect

Every 24 hours, Earth rotates on its axis. Half of the planet is heated every 12 hours, while the other half is in darkness. This is one of the main reasons Earth is heated unevenly. These differences in temperature create changes in air pressure that produce wind.

However, the winds do not blow in simple straight lines from high to low pressure, flowing up and down the globe. Instead, winds curve because our planet spins. This is called the **Coriolis Effect**. It bends every wind on Earth. Anywhere north of the equator, called the Northern Hemisphere, the winds blow to the right. Winds blow to the left anywhere south of the equator in the Southern Hemisphere.

WIND MAKES A HOME RUN

A batter in the major leagues has to watch the signs from the third-base coach. He also must be aware of wind conditions. If a batter has a 10-mile-per-hour (16-km) wind at his back, it will add about 30 extra feet (9 m) to a long fly ball. However, if that same wind is blowing in at the batter, it will shorten a fly ball by about 30 feet. That's enough of a difference to turn a home run into an out!

The strong winds from a hurricane cause ocean waters to rise many feet and then crash onto land in a powerful storm surge. A storm surge is often the most dangerous part of a hurricane because it creates massive flooding in low-lying areas. This cyclist is taking a huge risk by playing in the surf after a hurricane.

Naming Winds

The direction of the wind is based on the direction from which the wind is blowing. Easterly winds blow east to west. Westerly winds blow west to east.

We can depend upon particular wind patterns to stay the same in certain places of the world. Sailors and sea captains count on these winds remaining constant. For example, there are steady winds known as trade winds, named during the early days of sailing. Ships that traded goods between different countries knew they could get to their destination quicker when their sails caught hold of these winds. Another unique wind pattern is the doldrums. Sailors avoid this area north of the equator between the two trade winds because the winds there are often very light and calm. They can trap ships in one spot for weeks.

Sensing the Wind

There are ways you can accurately measure the direction and speed of the wind by using simple technology and your own five senses. For example, at airports, shipping ports, and seashores "wind socks" can show the direction of the wind. Perhaps you have seen these—they are often a bright, day-glow orange. A wind sock is tube shaped, with an open end and a closed end. It is usually attached to a pole that is planted in an open area. The wind blows into the open end of the sock, and it points the way the wind is blowing. The wind sock also gives a general sense of the speed of the wind. It flaps around gently in a light wind and stands in a straight line in a strong wind.

Another easy way to tell how fast the wind is blowing without any scientific tools is with the Beaufort scale. This scale was originally developed in 1806 by Admiral Sir Francis Beaufort and is still used today. By studying the effects of the wind on chimney smoke, trees, and leaves, you can estimate the speed of the wind.

CHINOOK WINDS

A chinook is a warm wind coming from the eastern slopes of the Rocky Mountains. Chinooks occur most often in winter and can warm temperatures more than 100 degrees in just a few hours. Typically, temperature change is around 40 degrees. Temperatures rapidly cool once a chinook leaves.

The Black Hills of South Dakota are home to the world's fastest recorded rise in temperature. After a chinook wind, the temperature there rose from −4°F (−20°C) to 45°F (7°C) in about 2 minutes. Several hours later, the chinook was gone. It took only 27 minutes for the temperatures to drop back down to −4°F.

The record for rapid temperature change in the United States is held by Great Falls, Montana, which on January 11, 1980, went from −32°F (0°C) to 15° F (−9°C), a 47-degree warm-up, in 7 minutes. That was because of a chinook. Chinooks are called "snow eaters" because of their ability to make snow melt rapidly.

The Birth of a Hurricane

During the day, land heats up quickly from the Sun's energy. At night, land also cools off quickly. The oceans are different. They take a bit longer to warm up, but once they do, oceans tend to stay warmer for a longer time than land does. This is the main reason why we have hurricanes. They get their power from the warm ocean water.

Hurricanes are tropical storms with very strong winds (over 74 miles or 119 km per hour). They form over the Atlantic Ocean

In August 2005, Hurricane Katrina struck the southern United States with winds reaching over 155 miles per hour (249 km). However, it was the storm surge from this powerful hurricane that devastated parts of Louisiana, Mississippi, and Alabama.

in tropical areas near Central Africa. As the warm ocean heats the air above it, high winds form. These high winds cause sea water to quickly evaporate into the air. As a result, the air contains a lot of warm water vapor, which rises into the air and condenses into clouds. This combination of heat and water creates huge, ferocious thunderstorms. When several thunderstorms clump together, the Coriolis Effect begins to spin them around as one enormous weather system.

When winds reach between 39 and 73 miles per hour (63 and 117 km), this weather system is classified as a tropical storm and is given a name. The high winds push this whole whirling thunderstorm across the ocean. It gathers more and more energy from warm, moist air and grows larger. Like the spinning of a top, the rotation of Earth twirls the storm faster and faster. Once the tropical storm reaches 74 miles per hour, a hurricane is born.

Rating a Hurricane's Intensity

The intensity of a hurricane is determined by its wind speed. The Saffir-Simpson scale uses five categories to rate a hurricane. A Category 1 is a mild hurricane and a Category 5 is the most severe. Under the right conditions, hurricanes can last for a few weeks, often wreaking havoc on the East and Gulf coasts of the United States and Mexico. Islands such as the Bahamas, Bermuda, and the Virgin Islands often endure the effects of hurricanes.

Much of the hurricane's destruction affects people living along the coasts. High winds create huge waves that swamp the shoreline, washing away homes, cars, and even people. These are called storm surges. Hurricane season begins June 1 and ends November 30. When a hurricane reaches cooler water or land, it loses its source of energy—heat—and quickly loses intensity.

This satellite photo of Hurricane Rita clearly shows the eye of this Category 5 hurricane. Hurricane Rita hit Louisiana and Texas only a month after Hurricane Katrina blasted through.

Strong winds are known by different names, depending on where they form. Hurricanes form in the Atlantic Ocean, typhoons in the Pacific Ocean, and cyclones in the Indian Ocean.

A Twister's Path

Tornadoes also form from cumulonimbus clouds, but over land instead of water. Some of these clouds become so massive that they create their own wind system within the cloud itself. A tornado forms when the winds inside the storm cloud start to rotate. This gives a tornado its telltale shape—a tall, whirling funnel of air, also known as a twister. Tornadoes can be over 500 feet (152 m) wide.

Inside the funnel, air spins at enormous speeds, up to 250 miles (402 km) per hour. Tornadoes average 20 to 50 miles (30–80 km) per hour as they move along the ground. The funnel acts like a giant vacuum cleaner that sucks up or destroys everything in its path. Although tornadoes usually only last about 15 minutes or less, they can travel several miles, destroying everything in their path. Because of their short lives, tornadoes are very hard to predict.

Tornadoes contain some of the fastest winds on Earth. They are known for picking up all kinds of objects, such as cows, cars, and tractor-trailers, before hurling them back to the ground. Strangely, sometimes these objects are unharmed. There are stories of tornadoes plucking all the feathers from a chicken while leaving the chicken alive.

Twisters are so short-lived that they are very difficult to predict. Many neighborhoods in Tornado Alley use sirens to warn of an approaching tornado, but this only gives people a few minutes warning, if that much!

Midwestern states in the United States have the distinction of having the highest number of destructive tornadoes in the world. This stretch of land is known as **Tornado Alley**. States such as Oklahoma, Kansas, and others in the Great Plains are very flat. This allows cold, dry, polar air flowing down from Canada to meet warm, moist, tropical air flowing up from the Gulf of Mexico. Tornadoes form when these cold and warm airs meet over Tornado Alley.

CHAPTER SIX

How to Forecast the Weather

"**I**f you don't like the weather, wait five minutes." This popular saying reflects the lack of control we really have over the weather. A basic understanding of the nature of clouds and wind can tell you what the weather will be like over the next few hours. With weather satellites, Doppler radar, and other sophisticated tools, today's meteorologists can predict the weather several days in advance. However, there is no such thing as forecasting, or predicting, the weather with 100% accuracy.

A Meteorologist's Work Is Never Done

There are many jobs for a meteorologist. You probably are most familiar with meteorologists on television. Most meteorologists work behind the scenes. For example, some work for the Tropical Prediction Center, part of the National Hurricane Center in Florida, tracking tropical storms and hurricanes. These meteorologists give people several days warning before a hurricane hits land. This saves many lives.

Other meteorologists develop new technology to measure and understand the weather. They may work for the U.S. government weather organization, the National Oceanic and Atmospheric Association (NOAA). The U.S. **National Weather Service** is a branch of NOAA and has its main weather station in Maryland. The NOAA has dozens of smaller stations all over the country. These stations collect information about local climates, among other important tasks, so that meteorologists can see long-term trends in the weather across the country.

However, without amateur meteorologists, the National Weather Service would not be able to understand the weather as efficiently as they do. Thousands of amateur observers across the country love measuring and recording the weather. They volunteer as part of the NOAA's Cooperative Observer Program. These weather buffs provide valuable daily and monthly information

MONITORING THE WIND

A wind sock tells you from which direction the wind is blowing. It also gives you an idea of how strong the wind is. To make your own wind sock, you will need:

- sleeve from a big, old, long-sleeved shirt
- wire
- needle and thread
- small rock or other weight
- string or twine

1. Cut one sleeve off the long-sleeved shirt. Bend the wire into a circle that is the same size as the top end of the sleeve (the end by the shoulder). Place the wire into this end of the sleeve, and attach it with a few stitches. This is the mouth of the wind sock.
2. Place the rock or weight on one edge of the wire. Sew it on tight to hold it in place. Tie the string onto the side of the wire opposite the rock.
3. Tie the other end of the string to a branch where it can move freely. The rock will keep the wind sock facing into the wind.
4. Now your wind sock is working. Use a compass to find out from which direction the wind is blowing.

A storm chaser is a person who pursues severe thunderstorms. Chasers are people from all walks of life, most of whom are very knowledgeable about meteorology. Contrary to Hollywood movies, chasers keep a safe distance of a mile or more from tornadoes.

to the NOAA on such things as rainfall, snowfall, temperatures, and river levels. In times of threatening weather, amateur weather observers have saved lives by quickly alerting the National Weather Service about local conditions.

Tools of the Trade

No matter if they are professionals or amateurs, meteorologists depend upon knowing the weather basics: temperature, air pressure, rainfall, and wind speed and direction. The main difference between meteorology in the 1800s and today is the level of detail. The same basic information about weather is collected and analyzed today as back then, but weather maps now allow meteorologists to know in great detail what the weather is doing and where it is doing it.

Technological inventions such as radar, satellites, and computers, just for starters, enable meteorologists to probe ever more deeply into this global phenomenon we experience as the weather.

The GOES-12 satellite shows Hurricane Rita swirling counter-clockwise in the Gulf of Mexico, before making landfall on the coast.

The best weather forecaster studies global weather patterns first, then focuses on to the entire United States, and finally looks at the weather that is happening locally. Most storms begin above 10,000 feet (3,048 m) and over an ocean. When a forecaster knows where a storm originates, she or he can track its course and predict where the storm will go over the next few days.

Technology allows forecasters the see this "big picture" of weather on a global and national scale. Doppler radar, radiosondes (instruments carried by weather balloons), satellites, and computers are some of the advanced scientific instruments used to collect this vital weather information across the entire planet.

Doppler Radar

RADAR is an acronym that stands for RAdio Detecting And Ranging. Early radar systems sent out powerful radio pulses that reflected off objects such as rain or clouds. The more rain or clouds, the more they reflected the radar signal. This told meteorologists about the location and size of certain weather events but not the speed and direction of the moving air.

Radar technology has developed quite a bit over the past 50 years. In the early 1990s, the NEXt Generation RADar system (NEXRAD) replaced the older Doppler radar systems. Throughout

Since 1995, this "Doppler on Wheels" mobile radar system has allowed adventurous scientists to drive directly into tornadoes. Maps are created from the Doppler images and have provided new insights into how tornadoes form and evolve.

The name TIROS stands for **T**elevision **I**nfra**R**ed **O**bservation **S**atellites. These satellites observe Earth's cloud cover and weather patterns from space.

the United States and overseas, there are about 159 NEXRAD Doppler radar stations. Doppler radars gather weather data and send it immediately to computers at the National Climatic Data Center (NCDC), a division of the National Weather Service. A map is generated that shows patterns of precipitation and its movement anywhere in the world. Updates are provided every five minutes. Doppler radar can show wind direction and speed more than 500 miles (805 km) away. Doppler radar also detects tornadoes *before* they form. Forecasters can now track storms days in advance, making Doppler radar an invaluable tool. Advance warnings of tornadoes and hurricanes have saved many lives.

Satellites

Satellites truly provide the biggest picture of Earth's weather. In 1960, the TIROS 1 satellite sent meteorologists the first photos of *all* Earth's clouds. Until this point, meteorologists could only see sections of the world's cloud cover. Since then, satellite technology has rapidly advanced, providing nearly complete coverage of the world's weather. Today, weather data from satellites is never more than six hours old.

Like Doppler radar, U.S. satellites look for storms that can threaten us. There are geostationary and polar-orbiting satellites beaming this information to weather stations all over the world. The United States, Japan, and Europe have geostationary satellites that orbit over the equator. They stay over the same spot while Earth is spinning. To do this, they need to be stationed about 22,000 miles (35,406 km) up to maintain just the right speed to keep up with Earth's rotation.

There are also two U.S. polar-orbiting satellites circling Earth from north to south, crossing over the South and North poles. They fly only about 530 miles (853 km) up in the atmosphere. Because Earth is rotating, these satellites capture images from

Twice a day, every day of the year, weather balloons are released simultaneously from almost 900 locations worldwide. The balloon flights last for about two hours. Weather balloons can drift as far as 125 miles (201 km) away and rise up to more than 20 miles (32 km) in the atmosphere.

every part of the planet every 12 hours. Information from satellites is channeled to a computer, along with information gathered from other meteorological instruments.

Radiosondes

Radiosondes are carried by weather balloons. Radiosondes allow scientists to measure winds and greatly improve our understanding of the weather.

Radiosondes that measure temperature, humidity, and pressure are attached to large balloons and released thousands of feet into the air. As the balloon rises higher in the sky, a radio transmitter sends the weather data to radiosonde stations on the ground. There are more than 900 radiosonde stations worldwide. When the balloon bursts, the weather instruments (which are wrapped together in a type of package) float to Earth on a parachute. The National Weather Service releases hundreds of radiosondes each day. About one-third of them are found, and returned. If you find one, you just drop it in a mailbox, postage free! Radiosondes were named for the word *sonde*, which is Old French for "sounding line."

Computers

Whether it comes from an amateur weather observer, a barometer, a satellite, or a weather balloon, every piece of weather information is fed into supercomputers at the National Weather Service. These supercomputers are able to compute more than 2 billion operations a second. Air pressure, Earth's rotation, the water cycle, and every other factor that completes the weather puzzle are fed into these computers. Weather maps are created that explain every weather action happening anywhere in the world *in that very instant.*

This process is also called numerical forecasting. Numerical forecasts allow weather forecasters to have an up-to-the-minute knowledge of the current weather. This greatly enhances their ability to predict the weather with as much accuracy as possible.

CHAPTER SEVEN

Is Our Climate Changing?

Just as our weather always changes, the climate of Earth has always changed as well. For example, ice ages blanketed parts of Earth with thick ice on and off for thousands of years. Volcanic eruptions have changed the climate in both directions. Molten lava can heat up a large area of the planet with its intense volcanic energy. Volcanic ash spewed miles into the sky can also block the Sun's rays, causing the world to become cold and uninhabitable. These cycles have been a part of Earth's natural history since the birth of the planet billions of years ago.

Earth has always balanced its temperature by sending the heat it receives from the Sun back out into space. However, certain gases in our atmosphere trap the heat that is given off from Earth's surface. These are called **greenhouse** gases, since they hold in heat like a greenhouse. Greenhouse gases, such as water vapor, carbon dioxide, methane, and nitrous oxide, are an important part of our atmosphere. They keep Earth from becoming a ball of ice with surface temperatures of about 0°F (–18°C).

Over the past century, many scientists have shown evidence that these greenhouse gases are building up. This buildup increases the amount of heat trapped close to the surface of

Air has no borders or immigration policy. We all breathe the same air. The pollution from a factory in the United States affects the air quality on the other side of the world, and vice versa.

Earth. Therefore, Earth is warming up. Many scientists believe human activities, including the burning of **fossil fuels**, are the cause. These fuels, mostly gas and oil, release carbon dioxide when they are burned. This is also called exhaust. The United States produces about 25% of the world's exhaust. Still, others say the increasing world temperatures are just a natural part of Earth's normal cycle.

Evidence of Global Warming?

The Intergovernmental Panel on Climate Change (IPCC) is a group of scientists from around the world who are brought together by the United Nations. Every year, this group meets to discuss recent scientific findings on climate change. They also debate how a warmer climate could affect our modern societies. Rising sea levels, melting polar ice and mountain **glaciers**, warmer oceans, and flooding are among the subjects of this scientific research on climate change.

Rising global temperatures are melting Earth's polar ice caps and glaciers and increasing the sea level. As global warming continues, millions of people are at risk from floods.

Sheets of thick ice called glaciers form on some mountains in various places of the world. These mountain glaciers have been slowly melting over the past 100 years. This melting of glacial ice has sharply increased over the past 30 years. The Arctic is also covered with thick sheets of ice. Today that ice is 40% thinner than it was just 30 years ago. Many scientists point out that rising global temperatures are the reason for this melting.

Sea levels around the world rose 4 to 8 inches (10–20 cm) during the twentieth century. Some of this increase is partly from the melting mountain glaciers. Many scientists believe that if the temperature keeps increasing, even more glacial ice will melt. One U.S. Environmental Protection Agency study foresees

THE HOLE IN THE OZONE

In addition to infrared light, the Sun sends ultraviolet (UV) light to Earth. Most of it is blocked by the ozone layer in the stratosphere. However, certain man-made chemicals destroy this protective ozone layer, which allows more UV light to reach the planet's surface. Because UV light is very harmful to living creatures and causes cancer, the use of these ozone-layer-destroying chemicals has been limited or banned since the 1980s. This has been a worldwide success, and today the "hole" in the ozone is shrinking.

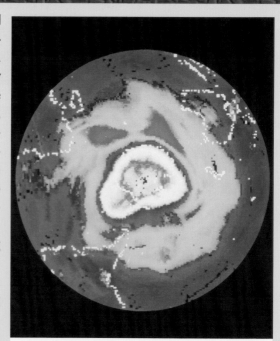

A satellite mapped the pink area outlined in white as a severe depletion, or "hole," in the ozone layer caused by pollution over Antarctica.

A warmer climate brings more rain to some parts of the world and less to others. The Amazon is now in its worst drought in 40 years.

a 1-foot (0.3-m) rise in sea levels on the Atlantic and Gulf coasts by 2050 and a 2-foot (0.6-m) rise by 2100. A 2-foot rise in the oceans would severely flood all coastal communities in the world. This much ocean water would also permanently cover a piece of the United States bigger than Massachusetts.

Evidence shows that ocean water is also heating up. Hurricanes receive their power from warm water. Based on computer models, some scientists say as the oceans heat up, the destructive strength of hurricanes will increase.

Scientists point out that it rains more now in certain areas of the world than it did 100 years ago. As temperatures rise, we could expect even more rainfall. Yet, scientists point out that other parts of the world will experience more **droughts**. There currently is not enough evidence to say whether drought is increasing or not.

A possible upside to **global warming** is having warmer winters. Although that means fewer snowball fights, it also means a longer growing season. This translates into more food production in certain areas of the world. There is already evidence in Europe that the growing season is several days longer since the 1960s. Spring plants now bloom about six days earlier.

It is important to remember that not all areas will have more food. If the world's temperatures keep increasing, those areas of the world that are already hot and dry will not be able to grow the same amount of food. Serious consequences will be felt in places such as the tropics and parts of Africa. Scientists predict that by the 2080s, about 80 million people, mostly within Africa, could go hungry because of climate change.

Humans Create Greenhouse Gases

Carbon dioxide gas is added to the atmosphere when fossil fuels are burned, such as gasoline and oil. Human activities use enormous amounts of these fuels. Each day, we use fossil fuels to power all parts of our lives. For example, every time you drive in a car, you are using fossil fuels. One way to slow climate change is to ride your bike more.

Carbon dioxide is removed from the air by plants during photosynthesis. When we cut down trees, we take away nature's ability to reduce carbon dioxide. Perhaps you can plant some trees to help reduce this greenhouse gas in our air.

HOW TO TEST AIR POLLUTION

Cut out a square piece of white cloth. Next, cut out a smaller square of cloth and glue it onto the middle of the first, larger square. Then, hang it outside for about a week. Peel off the square in the middle. Is the area underneath the smaller square cleaner than the surrounding cloth? Whatever made the cloth dirty is in the air that you breathe. Try placing the cloth in different locations, such as a park or near a factory. Notice if there are any differences.

The world's biggest contributors to greenhouse gas emissions, in particular the United States and Russia, did not sign the Kyoto Protocol. Many concerned citizens protested against their own governments in the hopes of changing this decision.

Thousands of people all around the world are changing the way they live in order to stop global warming. Most of the world's governments have pledged to switch to cleaner fuels, such as solar and wind energy. These do not release carbon dioxide into the air. Scientists are committed to researching new technologies and processes that do not put more greenhouse gases into our air.

The debate over global warming continues in scientific labs and governmental offices. Whether climate change is human-made or a natural cycle of Earth's weather is still not completely understood. However, the evidence points out that the world's climate is shifting. The effects are visible. Perhaps we should remember a most important thing: We all can make a difference in our world.

Glossary

air – the mixture of gases that form the atmosphere of Earth

air pollution – chemicals or substances in the atmosphere that are directly or indirectly harmful to living things

air pressure – the weight of air pressing down on Earth. Air pressure can change from place to place, and this causes air to move, flowing from areas of high pressure toward areas of low pressure. It is the same as barometric pressure.

atmosphere – the layer of gases surrounding a planet. Earth's atmosphere is divided into five layers: troposphere, stratosphere, mesosphere, thermosphere, and exosphere.

barometer – an instrument that measures air pressure

blizzard – an intense winter storm where winds of 35 miles per hour or higher blow falling snow. In a blizzard, you cannot see farther than one-quarter mile for at least three hours.

breeze – a light wind

climate – the average weather conditions in a certain place or during a certain season. Weather may change from day to day, but climate changes only over hundreds or thousands of years. Many animals and plants can survive in only one kind of climate.

condensation – the change of water vapor to liquid water, forming clouds, fog, or dew

Coriolis Effect – a force that redirects moving objects in relation to Earth's rotation. The object is still going straight, but Earth moves beneath it, which makes it look as though an object is veering to one side. In the Northern Hemisphere, Earth rotates west to east, so winds and currents are deflected to the right in the Northern Hemisphere. In the Southern Hemisphere, they appear to move to the left.

drizzle – a light rain made up of very small water droplets

drought – a period when a region has little rainfall. Droughts can affect a small area for a season or an entire continent for years. Too little rainfall can cause shortages in the water supply, destroy crops, and cause widespread hunger. Droughts also dry up soil, which then gets picked up by the wind and causes dust storms.

equator – the imaginary line that circles the middle of Earth like a belt. It separates the Northern Hemisphere from the Southern Hemisphere.

evaporation – the process of changing a liquid (such as water) to a vapor. It is the opposite of condensation.

flood – when rivers rise and go over their banks after days of heavy rain and/or melting snows. A flash flood is sudden flooding that occurs when floodwaters rise swiftly with no warning within several hours of an intense rain. They often occur after intense rainfall from slow-moving thunderstorms.

fog – a cloud on the ground that reduces visibility. Dense fog can reduce visibility while driving so that you cannot see farther than one-quarter mile, which creates travel problems and delays.

fossil fuels – the remains of ancient plants and animals that turn into oil and gas over millions of years

freeze – when the temperature falls below 32 degrees Fahrenheit over a large area for an extended time. A freeze can destroy crops.

glacier – a large sheet of ice that survives for thousands of years

global warming – the theory that increased concentrations of greenhouse gases are causing Earth's surface temperature to rise

greenhouse – the heating effect of Earth's atmosphere. The atmosphere acts like a greenhouse because sunlight freely passes through it and warms the surface. As Earth sends heat back toward space, some of the heat is trapped by the atmosphere, which keeps Earth at a comfortable temperature.

high pressure – a whirling mass of cool, dry air that generally brings fair weather and light winds. When viewed from above, winds spiral out of a high-pressure center in a clockwise rotation in the Northern Hemisphere. These bring sunny skies.

humidity – the amount of water vapor in the air

hurricane – an intense storm with swirling winds up to 156 miles per hour. Usually around 300 miles across, hurricanes can be 1,000 to 5,000 times larger than tornadoes.

hurricane season – a six-month period from June 1 to November 30, when conditions are favorable for hurricane development

low pressure – a whirling mass of warm, moist air that generally brings stormy weather with strong winds. When viewed from above, winds spiral into a low-pressure center in a counterclockwise rotation in the Northern Hemisphere.

meteorologist – a scientist who studies and predicts the weather. Meteorologists use sophisticated equipment, such as Doppler radar and supercomputers, but they also rely on old-fashioned sky watching.

meteorology – the study of the atmosphere and all its phenomena, including weather and how to forecast it.

mist – water droplets so small that they are floating in the air. Because mist droplets do not fall, mist is a type of fog.

monsoon – a seasonal wind, found especially in Asia, that reverses direction between summer and winter and often brings heavy rains

National Weather Service – the federal agency that provides weather, hydrologic, and climate forecasts and warnings for the United States

ozone – a form of oxygen that has a weak chlorine odor. Ozone heats the upper atmosphere by absorbing ultraviolet rays from sunlight. In the troposphere, ozone is a pollutant, but in the stratosphere, it filters out harmful ultraviolet radiation.

precipitation – the general name for water in any form falling from clouds. This includes rain, drizzle, hail, snow, and sleet. Dew, frost, and fog are not considered precipitation.

smog – visible air pollution in urban areas that looks like dirty fog in large cities

storm – any disturbed state of the atmosphere that creates unpleasant weather such as rain, lightning, thunder, hail, snow, sleet, and freezing rain

Sun – The star in the center of our solar system. The Sun is responsible for most of Earth's weather, even though it is 93 million miles away. The Sun's intense heat gives energy to Earth's atmosphere and sets it in motion.

temperature – the measurement of how hot or cold something is

thermometer – an instrument that measures temperature

thunder – the explosive sound of air expanding as it is heated by lightning. This air is about 54,000 degrees Fahrenheit.

thunderstorm – a storm produced by a cumulonimbus cloud that always has lightning and thunder. Rain, hail, high winds, and tornadoes may or may not occur.

Tornado Alley – the region of the United States where tornadoes occur most frequently. Tornado Alley is the corridor along the Great Plains. It extends from the Rocky Mountains in the West to the Appalachian Mountains in the East.

Bibliography

Keen, Richard A. *Skywatch: The Western Weather Guide*. Fulcrum Publishing: Golden, Colo., 1987.

Kloesel, Dr. Kevin. "At ARM's Length: Using Radiosondes to Extend Our Grasp of Weather and Climate." Climate Education Update (newsletter).

Kristof, Nicholas D. 2005. "The Storm Next Time." *The New York Times*, 2005.

Lagassé, Paul (Ed.). *The Columbia Encyclopedia*, Sixth Edition. Columbia University Press: New York, 2000.

"National Climatic Data Center: Protecting the Past, Revealing the Future." NOAA Satellite and Information Service.
www.ncdc.noaa.gov/oa/ncdc.html

"Public Awareness: Satellites and Hurricane Hunters." Department of Atmospheric Sciences.
ww2010.atmos.uiuc.edu/(Gh)/guides/mtr/hurr/awar.rxml

Wagner, Ronald L. and Bill Adler, Jr. *The Weather Sourcebook*. Adler & Robin Books: Washington, D.C., 1997.

"Weather and Climate Basics." The National Center for Atmospheric Research.
eo.ucar.edu/basics/index.html

Williams, Jack. *The Weather Book. An Easy-to-Understand Guide to the USA's Weather*. Random House: New York, 1997.

Further Exploration

BOOKS

Blanchard, Duncan C. *Snowflake Man: A Biography of Wilson A. Bentley*. Newark, Ohio: McDonald and Woodward Publishing Company, 1998.

Demarest, Chris L. *Hurricane Hunters! Riders on the Storm*. New York: Margaret K. McElderry, 2006.

Libbrecht, Ken. *Ken Librecht's Field Guide to Snowflakes*. Stillwater, Minn.: Voyageur Press, 2006.

Vogel, Carole G. *Weather Legends: Native American Lore and the Science of Weather*. Brookfield, Conn.: The Millbrook Press, 2001.

Williams, Jack. *The Weather Book: An Easy-to-Understand Guide to the USA's Weather*. New York: Random House, 1997.

WEB SITES

ametsoc.org
The American Meteorological Society

www.cpc.ncep.noaa.gov
Climate Prediction Center

eo.ucar.edu/kids/links.html#science
Everything about the weather, including activities, links, glossary

www.extremescience.com/mainweather.htm
Extreme weather record breakers

ncdc.noaa.gov/oa/climate
Weather satellite data and information from the National Climatic Data Center

www.nhc.noaa.gov
Hurricane Central from the Tropical Prediction Center of the National Weather Service

www.nws.noaa.gov
The National Weather Service

www.nws.noaa.gov/om/coop
The National Weather Service's Cooperative Observer Program

www.rcn27.dial.pipex.com/cloudsrus/home.html
Everything about the weather, including activities, links, glossary

www.tornadoproject.com
The Tornado Project

weather.yahoo.com
Worldwide five-day forecasts

www.weatherwizkids.com
Includes facts, folklore, games, jokes, experiments, and activities

www.wildwildweather.com
Everything about the weather, including activities, links, glossary

yosemite.epa.gov/oar/globalwarming.nsf/content/index.html
Global warming site

Index

Page numbers for illustrations are in *italic*

About the Author

RANDI MEHLING is the author of several nonfiction books for young readers. She has written on a wide variety of health and science topics, including *Great Extinctions of the Past* and this book in Chelsea House's Scientific American series. Mehling has a passion for the natural world and our relationship with it. She is a published poet and essayist and holds a masters degree in public health.

Picture Credits